THE BOOK ON SAFE DRIVING

50 Quick Tips to Keep Yourself,
Your Family, and Your Employees
Safer On The Road

Joe Darden

Visit our Web site: www.joedardengroup.com

First published in the United States of America by
Joe Darden Group, LLC
9220 SW Barbur Blvd #119-146
Portland, OR 97219
503-367-7643

ISDN 9780615247373

QUM 10 9 8 7 6 5 4 3 2

Book Design: Brian Thomas Wright Creative Group
Cover, Interior Layout and Illustrations: Canyon Scharf

Printed in the United States of America

This book is available at special quantity discounts to use as premiums, or for use in corporate training programs. For more information please write to the Joe Darden Group at book@joedardengroup.com.

FIRST EDITION

Joe Darden Group and The SMART Driving System are Trademarks of the Joe Darden Group. The SMART Driving System is also a registered copyright.

Dedicated to my son, Eric and my wife, Jan.
The reasons I choose to drive SMART.

CONTENTS

SHATTERED CALM

The crash occurred on Friday, July 11, 2003 at about 10:00 a.m. The roadway was dry, the sky was clear and there were no problems with visibility. It was a bright, beautiful summer day, a calm day that was about to be shattered by a fatal traffic collision.

The following account details that crash, a crash that involved a UPS driver. In July of 2003, I worked for UPS and was deeply involved in the investigation of this crash.

The collision occurred on a straight, two-lane stretch of road divided by a solid, double yellow line. The UPS driver was delivering a route in a rural part of Oregon. He had left the UPS center around 9:00 a.m. and had made about three of his 80 deliveries prior to the crash. He was driving the typical mid-sized UPS delivery vehicle just like the one that probably delivers to your home or workplace.

During an interview after the crash, the driver stated that he was driving at or below the posted speed limit of 55 MPH while heading to his next delivery stop. He was about one mile away from that stop; the farthest thing from his mind was that he would not make it that last mile. The driver stated that he noticed a small red sedan heading toward him in the opposite lane, but that he did not notice anything unusual about that vehicle. That is, until the other vehicle swerved across the double, yellow line into his lane of travel for about one second and then swerved back into its own lane. This occurred while the two vehicles were still about 200 to 300 yards away from each other. At that point, the driver stated, he slowed in response to the unusual action and began to focus more of his attention on the oncoming vehicle. About five seconds later, just as the two vehicles were about to pass, the red sedan swerved again and struck the UPS vehicle head-on.

I remember the details of this crash so vividly because I was the driver behind the wheel of the UPS vehicle. The red sedan swerved into my lane so fast that I only had time to think, "This guy's going to hit me!" I didn't have time to even think about swerving off the road to try to avoid the collision. I later found out that there was no shoulder on the side of the road. If I had been able to swerve, my UPS vehicle would likely have rolled over because of the abrupt edge.

To this day, I can still remember the feeling of the wind hitting my face as both of the front windshields of the UPS truck flew out from the force of the impact. I can still remember that it was the loudest and most violent event that I had ever experienced. I can still remember the vehicles coming to a stop, hearing the hiss of steam and seeing smoke rising from the front of the UPS vehicle. I can still remember looking down out of the driver's side door and seeing the oil from the diesel engine flowing away from the vehicles toward the ditch on the opposite side of the road and thinking, "The truck is bleeding." And I can still remember the next thoughts I had, "Hey, I'm still alive" and then, "Hey, I'm still conscious." It was then, probably about five to ten seconds after the vehicles came to a stop, that I started thinking about all of those TV shows and movies that I had watched over the years and how big car crashes lead to big car fires and explosions. Those visuals, coupled with the smoke and hissing sounds coming from the front of the vehicle, encouraged me to get away from the two vehicles as quickly as possible. It was at that point that I reached down, unbuckled my seat belt and walked away from the crash.

The crash occurred about 20 yards away from a house. By the time I walked across the road, the owner of that house was walking toward me while talking on a phone with the 9-1-1 dispatcher. As I looked to my right I saw a woman walking up to me asking if I was OK. I later found out that she had been driving the vehicle directly behind the red sedan. I told her, "I think I'm OK." They both said that I should probably sit down and the owner of the house brought out a folding chair so I wouldn't have to sit in the dirt. Once I sat down, I started looking myself over for injuries. I had cuts on both of my knees, and I was moving a little stiffly, but I did not notice any severe pain. About that time (two to three minutes after the crash) two men pulled up behind my UPS vehicle and went forward to check on the driver of the other vehicle. One of the men commented on the fire that had started underneath the vehicles and asked if anyone had a fire extinguisher. I told him that there was a fire extinguisher in the cab of the UPS vehicle. He grabbed the extinguisher and put out the flames before the fire could spread.

The owner of the house let me use his phone so I could call my center manager and tell him about the crash. Over the phone I described what had happened and told him that the police and fire department were on their way to the crash scene. My manager asked if I was OK. Again, I said, "I think so, but my knees are bleeding." He asked if the driver of the other vehicle was OK as well. I told him, "I don't think he could have survived the crash." My manager asked incredulously, "Are you serious!?" I said, "Yes." Later, when I discussed that conversation with my manager, he stated that I had been so calm and matter-of-fact on the phone that he hadn't realized how severe the crash had actually been. He told me he would have expected someone to be hysterical in that situation.

My manager said that he had to make some calls to get some UPS people to the crash scene and that he would be there as soon as possible. A few moments later, the police, fire department and ambulance arrived. The police officer asked me some questions about the crash and checked on the driver of the other vehicle. The paramedics checked me over, asked me some more questions and loaded me up for the trip to the hospital.   On the way to the hospital, I called my wife to let her know what had happened. When my wife asked, the paramedic in the ambulance confirmed that the driver of the red sedan had not survived the collision.

Upon my arrival at the hospital, I was thoroughly checked over to make sure I did not have any hidden or more severe injuries. I was also given some medication for the pain and swelling and one of my knees was stitched up. I also had to have one of my knees stitched up. As it turns out, my right knee had struck the ignition key during the impact and my left knee had hit the switch for the headlights.

During this time, I had my second interview with a police officer, a county Sheriff's Deputy. The deputy asked me if I would consent to a test to confirm that there were no drugs or alcohol in my system. Since I don't drink or use drugs, I had no problem submitting to the test. Soon after, I was asked to submit to a similar test by a UPS representative. This was when I started to realize there was going to be a great deal of investigation to help determine the circumstances surrounding the collision. Fortunately for me, I was not doing anything that I should have not been doing prior to the crash. I was not speeding, talking on the phone or being distracted by anything inside or outside the cab. Nor was I under the influence of any drugs, alcohol or medication when the crash occurred.

Once the tests were completed and I was cleared for release, my wife drove me home so I could begin recuperating. Later that evening, four people from UPS came to my house to get a statement concerning the crash; three were UPS managers and one was a fellow UPS driver who was the Union Shop Steward. Again, I was asked to recount the events leading up to and after the crash. They asked me to call the insurance company and give them a detailed account of the crash. It took about an hour or so to finish the call to the insurance company and the interview with the representatives from UPS. As they were leaving, the Union representative pointed out to me that my hands were shaking while I was talking about the crash. I looked down at my hands and said, "Yeah, that's weird, they start shaking every time I talk about it." For the next two days, anytime I talked about the crash, my hands would start shaking.

The Monday after the crash occurred, I was back at work. Needless to say, I was in no condition to head out and deliver packages. Both of my knees were stiff, my back was hurting, and my chest and abdomen were sore. They showed significant bruising from the seat/shoulder belt. Regardless of my injuries, I would not have been allowed to drive because of the continuing investigation. UPS assigned a safety manager from a different state to help ensure an unbiased investigation. In addition, the insurance company that UPS uses also sent an agent to investigate the collision. Both investigators interviewed me separately which meant I had to tell the story yet again. Later, the company that insured the red sedan also questioned me.

I was also able to address the other UPS drivers at my center during the Monday morning meeting and tell them what had happened. I told them that wearing my seat belt and having the bulkhead door (the one that leads from the cab of the UPS vehicle back to the cargo area) closed undoubtedly saved me from more severe injuries and possibly from dying in the crash. Had I not been wearing my seat belt, I have no doubt that I would have either been thrown out of the vehicle or thrown into the dash, steering wheel and/or windshield frame. Furthermore, if I had not had my bulkhead door closed, packages, my hand truck, or anything else that was in the cargo area could have flown into the cab striking me with the force of the collision. During one of the interviews, I was told that it took the investigators over 30 minutes to pry open the bulkhead door so they could get into the cargo area. All of the packages in the rear of the vehicle had slid forward during the collision, and many were wedged up against the bulkhead door.

Ultimately, all the investigations showed that there was nothing I could have done to avoid the collision. The speedometer of the UPS vehicle I was driving had broken during the crash and the needle was locked at 38 MPH. The skid marks and crash scene photos showed that the vehicle I was driving never crossed out of its lane. They did reveal that the driver of the red sedan never applied the brakes or tried to avoid the collision. The woman that witnessed the crash from behind the red sedan confirmed the statements I had given to the police, fire department, UPS and the insurance companies.

I have replayed that morning over and over again in my head and still do not see any way that I could have avoided the crash. Neither could I identify anything I had done incorrectly that contributed to it. This more than anything else is probably what has allowed me to move on emotionally. More than one UPS driver has told me that they probably wouldn't be able to drive a UPS vehicle again after an accident involving a fatality. I have, in fact, heard stories of UPS drivers who quit their jobs after they were involved in a crash resulting in a fatality. In some cases, the driver not only quit driving for UPS, he quit driving altogether.

At the time, I felt fortunate that I had not been more severely injured than I was. I was also glad that I had long ago adopted the safe driving practices that helped me survive this crash. I had about one second to react from the time the red sedan crossed into my lane until the crash occurred. I did not have time to put on my seat belt or to close my bulkhead door. The fact that I always wore my seat belt and I always kept my bulkhead door closed when I was driving helped me survive physically. The fact that I was not distracted or doing something that I shouldn't have been doing behind the wheel helped me to move on emotionally without always wishing I could have done something different.

It's impossible for me to go through a situation like this and not ask the "What if?" questions. What if I had not been driving that day? What if I had taken a different route? What if I had taken longer at a previous delivery? Eventually I began to feel that, if the crash had to occur, I was probably the best person to be involved. On that particular day, I was delivering that specific route because the regular driver had taken a day off. If the regular UPS driver had not taken the day off, he may have been involved in the crash, may have been more severely injured, or he could have had a harder time dealing with the crash emotionally. If I had not been on the road it's possible the red sedan may have hit the next vehicle on the roadway. The next vehicle behind mine was the sedan with the two men who used the fire extinguisher from the UPS truck. I doubt that sedan would have been able to handle the impact as well as the UPS vehicle simply due to the difference in vehicle sizes.

To this day, I still do not know what caused the driver of the red sedan to cross over the center lines and hit my vehicle head-on. I do know that I am grateful to have learned and applied the safe driving practices that allowed me to walk away from that terrible crash. So when people ask, "Why is safe driving important to me?" I tell them, "Because it's personal." I am walking, talking, living proof that safe driving practices can not only make your everyday commute safer and less stressful, they can also protect you from serious injury or death when something goes terribly wrong. Fortunately for everyone, it's not difficult to apply the safe driving principles I will discuss in this book. It's simply a matter of choice. A driver chooses how he is going to drive every time he gets behind the wheel. I'm glad I made the right choices on July 11, 2003. Now, let's discuss the choices you can make everyday.

CHOICES

C hoice is something that every driver has when operating a vehicle. Drivers can choose to talk on their cell phone when they are driving, or not. They can choose to send text messages while they are driving (yes, people really do this), or not. Drivers can choose to reach into the glove compartment, read a book, change the CD or select a different file on the MP3 player while they are driving, or not. But these are all choices that are completely (100%) up to the driver. Many of the collisions that are happening on our roadways today are happening because a driver has made the wrong choice. Sure, you will hear reasons like, "The road was wet," "It was dark," or "I didn't see the other car until it was too late." But, at the end of the day, it is almost always a wrong choice about driving behavior that is the root cause of traffic crashes.

You have already made a choice by picking up this book. Your choice now is whether to continue reading and to apply the proven techniques described herein to your own driving methods, or not. Again, it is a choice that is completely up to you as a driver. I will never make the claim that applying all these techniques will guarantee that you will never be involved in a traffic collision. However, I will say that consistently applying the techniques in this book and making a conscious effort to develop safe driving habits will not only reduce the likelihood that you will be involved in a crash, but will also make you a more relaxed, more confident and a more prepared driver.

Drivers of all experience levels can apply the techniques described in this book. The quick, "common sense" tips and techniques can be used to help start new drivers off on the right foot by establishing a solid foundation of safe driving habits. They can also be used by more experienced drivers to supplement their current defensive driving practices. See how many of these principles you already apply when you're behind the wheel and choose the new principles you might want to adopt.

WHAT IS SMART™ DRIVING?

Throughout this book, I will refer to SMART™ Driving and I thought it would be a good idea to provide a definition before the 50 driving tips. Simply put, SMART™ is an acronym for the driving system I created to aid in the instruction and retention of defensive driving principles. Each letter of the acronym (shown below) represents one of the five main concepts of the SMART Driving System™. While this book does not go into in-depth detail for each of the five main concepts, many of the key principles of the program are discussed within the tips.

SMART ™ **DRIVING SYSTEM**

Study

Maintain

Anticipate

Respond

Train

Tip One
Back That Up!

1. Back into parking spots whenever possible.

Whenever possible, back into your parking spot. This simple technique allows you to visually clear the area that you are backing into. After you have visually cleared the area, you can immediately back and park before the situation gets a chance to change.

When you return to your vehicle and are ready to leave, you will have much better visibility looking out of your front windshield than you would if you were backing out. Typically you will be able to exit your parking spot more quickly and safely than if you had to back out. Remember, at some point while you are parking, you are going to have to back your vehicle anyway. So ask yourself, is it safer to back into an open parking spot, one that you just visually cleared and know is not likely to change, or is it safer to back from that parking spot into a busy parking lot or traffic situation that is constantly changing? Which technique gives you the best visibility? Which technique minimizes the chance of a backing collision? Professional drivers are instructed to back first because it reduces the likelihood of a backing crash.

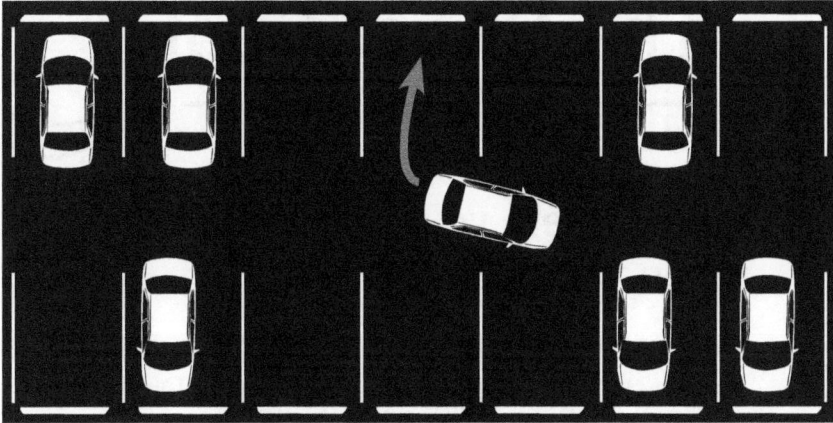

Did you know?

Based on a report by the 2006 Motor Vehicle Crash Data from FARS and GES, there were approximately 190,000 backing crashes reported in 2006. The actual number of backing crashes is likely much higher because of the many unreported backing crashes that occur annually.

Tip Two
The Sweet Spot

2. Know where your rear bumper is when you back up.

The Sweet Spot

Using the "Sweet Spot" technique allows the driver to consistently know where his rear bumper is while backing into a parking space.

This technique is easier to learn if you have someone assist you the first time you try it, but it can be done even if you are alone. The idea is to identify the "Sweet Spot" on your vehicle that lines up with a line or curb behind your vehicle when backing. This Sweet Spot will let you know when your rear bumper is even with that line or curb. It may sound a little complicated but it's actually quite easy. First, have your assistant stand behind and beside the rear of your vehicle, on the driver's side, where he is safely out of the way, but where you can still see and hear him clearly. Next, back your vehicle until your assistant tells you that your rear bumper is even with the curb, sidewalk or line that you do not want to cross. Once you have stopped and secured your vehicle in the desired location, look over your left shoulder through the driver's side rear window (if equipped) and locate the boundary that you do not want your rear bumper to cross. Finally, identify where that boundary lines up with the bottom of your driver's side rear window. That spot is your Sweet Spot; if you remember where that spot is on the bottom of your driver's side rear window and use that Sweet Spot every time you are backing up to a boundary, it will help you stop your vehicle in the desired location. I always tell participants learning my SMART Driving System™, that every backing crash involving a stationary object that has ever occurred happened because someone backed up just a little too far. Using the Sweet Spot technique can help keep you from making that same mistake.

The Sweet Spot – Inside

Here is the view from inside the vehicle. Note how the "Sweet Spot" lines up with the curb. Learning to apply this simple technique will help you identify where your rear bumper is while you are backing.

Tip Three
None For The Road

3. Don't drink and drive.

This tip is so basic and so fundamental to driving SMART that I almost didn't even include it in this book. However, there are still people who die every day in motor vehicle crashes caused by drivers who are under the influence. On the off chance that you have not already heard this message countless time, do not drink and drive and never ride in a vehicle with someone who has been drinking. If drivers would follow this one, simple rule, thousands of lives would be saved every year.

Tip Four
Plan Ahead

4. One of the best ways to drive SMART is to plan ahead and prepare yourself anytime you are going to get behind the wheel of a vehicle.

Know Your Route.

Think about your planned route and identify any potential hazards or delays. These could include: construction zones, "bottlenecks," rough roads, blind corners, hidden intersections or any area that you know frequently causes problems for other motorists. Many metropolitan areas provide online or mobile phone updates of current traffic conditions. Checking these resources before you leave can help you plan your route to avoid congested areas. Planning your route can also help you save money by eliminating multiple trips and double-backs. Rather than making several short trips to run errands during the day, plan one trip that takes you to each of your destinations without having to double back. This planning will save you time as well as fuel. You can even plan details like eliminating left turns across traffic by setting up as many right turns as possible on your route.

Planning Checklist

Plan Your Route:

_____

_____

☐ **Traffic Congestion** _____

☐ **Construction Zones** _____

☐ **Rough Roads** _____

☐ **Dangerous Intersections** _____

☐ **Known Problem Areas** _____

Local Number for Current Traffic Conditions:

_____

Did you know?

A little time spent planning ahead can save a driver hours of commuting throughout the year.

Tip Five
Don't Drive Blind

5. Check your blind spot

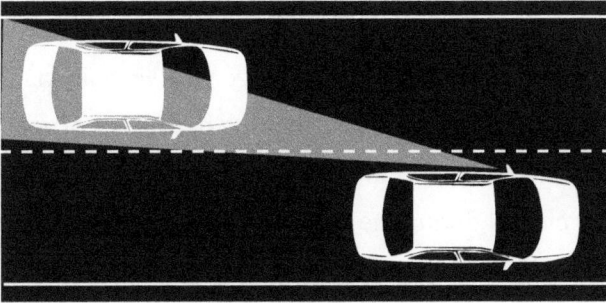

K now what is going on in the space that you are going to enter. Whether you are changing lanes in traffic or pulling away from the curb, taking a quick look over your shoulder will allow you to "visually clear" your blind spot and make a safer transition into your new lane of travel. Most everyone does a good job of checking their blind spot when they are driving in traffic. However, many people rely on their mirrors too much when pulling away from a curb. Checking your blind spot in these situations will not only allow you to see traffic in the lane of travel that you are going to enter, but it will also allow you to "visually clear" traffic that may be entering from a side street or driveway that is also in your blind spot.

Tip Six
Check Your Car's "Eyes"

6. Clean your headlights and make sure they are adjusted or "aimed" properly

One of the easiest ways to maximize your visibility during low-light conditions is to make sure that the headlights of your vehicle are aimed properly and that they are free of road film and dirt. This is especially critical during the winter months when there are fewer hours of daylight. Also during this time of the year there is often water on the roadway causing tire spray, which can quickly contribute to road film forming on your headlights. It's easy to check, and easy to correct. Simply wipe your finger across your headlights and see if there is any film that has collected. If there is, wipe if off with a damp cloth or towel. Have your headlights checked by a qualified mechanic to verify that they are properly aimed. This will ensure that the beams of the headlights are illuminating the desired areas ahead of your vehicle when driving at night.

Tip Seven
Keep Your
Car Happy

7. Maintain your vehicle

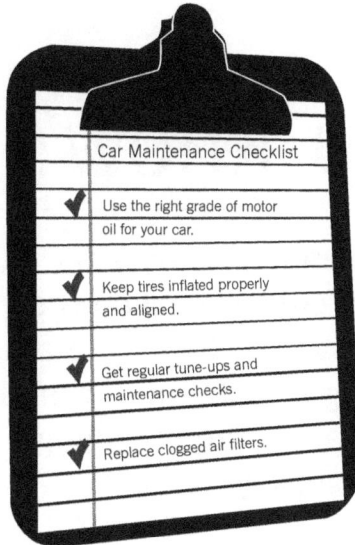

Car Maintenance Checklist

- ✔ Use the right grade of motor oil for your car.
- ✔ Keep tires inflated properly and aligned.
- ✔ Get regular tune-ups and maintenance checks.
- ✔ Replace clogged air filters.

Keep on top of preventative maintenance to help ensure that your vehicle is safe to operate and to minimize the chance that you will find yourself stranded at the side of the road. Simple things like tire pressure and fluid level monitoring can be done at home. If you are mechanically inclined, you may wish to perform engine oil changes yourself. Otherwise, it is a good idea to find a good local mechanic (preferably one who has been referred by someone you trust) or to use the service shop at the local dealer for your vehicle. Most vehicles come with a booklet that shows a maintenance schedule. Some vehicle manufacturers incorporate the schedule of maintenance into the owner's manual. If you do not have the maintenance schedule for your vehicle, you can contact your dealer's maintenance department or you may be able to download it from your vehicle manufacturer's website.

Did you know?

Preventative maintenance pays for itself over time by reducing costly breakdowns. It also increases driver safety. Changing a tire in your garage or noticing a problem in time to take it to a shop is far safer than changing a tire at the edge of a busy roadway.

Tip Eight
Keep It Straight

8. Keep your wheels straight while waiting to make a turn

This is an easy safe driving habit to develop, but it is often overlooked simply because drivers are never told why it's important. The question to ask is, "What would happen if I was struck from behind?" If the wheels of your vehicle are already turned and you are struck from behind, you will be forced into the path of oncoming traffic. This could make an already bad situation much worse by increasing the severity of the collision and involving other motorists in the crash. If the wheels are still pointed straight ahead and your vehicle is struck from behind, it is less likely that your vehicle will be forced into oncoming traffic.

Keep it Straight

What would happen to a vehicle waiting to make a left turn at this intersection if it was struck from behind and its wheels were already turned to the left?

Tip Nine
Pre-Trip

9. Pre-trip your vehicle

- [ ] **1. Check the condition of the tires**
    - [ ] **Inflation**
    - [ ] **Cuts**
    - [ ] **Tread**

- [ ] **2. Fluid Leaks**

- [ ] **3. Lights and signals are working properly**

- [ ] **4. Hazard or breakdown warning signs**

- [ ] **5. Follow a routine**

    - **Start and finish at the same point each time**

    - **Mark a scheduled Pre-Trip on the calendar**

For years, operators of commercial vehicles have been required to perform a "Pre-Trip" anytime they are going to operate a vehicle. Simply put, a Pre-Trip is giving the vehicle a quick, visual inspection to make sure that it is safe to operate. Operators of commercial vehicles are required to do this daily. As operators of non-commercial vehicles, the general public is not required to perform daily Pre-Trips, but it is always a good idea to check the condition of your vehicle on a regular basis anyway. During a Pre-Trip, you should be checking the condition of the tires (inflation, cuts, tread), checking for fluid leaks, verifying that all required lights and signals are working properly and looking for anything that could cause a hazard or breakdown while you are driving. As stated earlier, a Pre-Trip is not required for personal vehicles, but any motor vehicle operator can be cited for operating a vehicle that is not safe for the road. To help make a Pre-Trip easier and more effective, the vehicle operator should conduct it the same way each time. Have a routine and follow that routine. Start and finish at the same point each time so you will be more likely to notice changes that have occurred since your last inspection. It's also a good idea to schedule your Pre-Trip on your calendar or day planner to make sure that you remember to perform the vehicle inspection on a regular basis.

Did you know?

Having a Pre-Trip routine can help prevent traffic citations and even crashes that result from faulty equipment.

Tip Ten
Front Space Cushion

10. Keep a vehicle length between your vehicle and the vehicle ahead of you when stopped in traffic

This is a fundamental rule of SMART Driving. A "vehicle length" does not mean to leave so much space that another vehicle may enter that area. It means leaving enough space to keep your options open. Keeping a vehicle length between your vehicle and the vehicle in front of you does four things to help keep you safe:

1. If the vehicle in front of you stalls and cannot move, you can safely maneuver your vehicle around the stalled vehicle without having to back up in traffic.

2. If the vehicle in front of you starts to roll backward before moving forward, it will be less likely to roll back into your vehicle.

3. When the vehicle in front of you does pull away from the stop, you will already have some of the space cushion necessary for a safe following distance.

4. Finally, and most importantly, if your vehicle is struck from behind, you will be less likely to be forced into the vehicle in front of you. This is important because, if you strike the vehicle in front of you, there will be additional damage to your vehicle. Also, depending upon the circumstances of the collision, your insurance may be responsible to cover some or all of the damages to the vehicle that your vehicle struck.

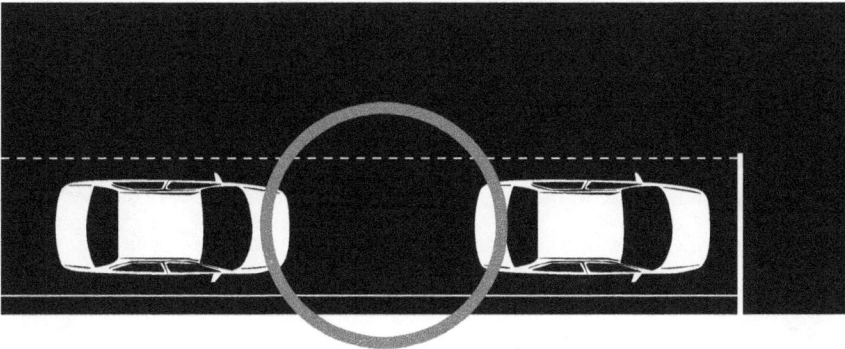

Tip 11
Driver Maintenance

11. Maintain yourself

J ust as vehicle maintenance is very important, driver maintenance is also a critical element of defensive driving.

1. Make sure that you get adequate rest before driving. Studies have shown that the effects of driving while drowsy are very similar to driving while intoxicated. Both conditions cause a delay in reaction time, limiting a person's ability to quickly anticipate and respond to changing situations.

2. Read the instructions on prescription and over-the-counter medications. Many of these labels specifically instruct the user to avoid driving while taking the medication because it may cause drowsiness and impair response time. There is also a concern when taking multiple medications that may have adverse interactions with each other. If in doubt, a driver should consult his doctor.

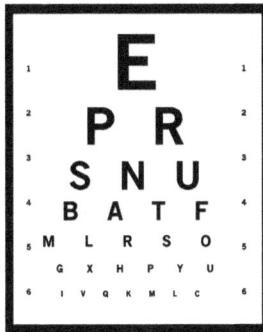

3. If you wear corrective lenses, be sure to get regular eye exams to help ensure that you are wearing the correct prescription. This, obviously, will help you to identify hazards from a distance and help you avoid emergency situations.

Tip 12
What's Going On?

12. Study your surroundings

1. Do not just look around while you are driving. You must actively search and study what is going on around your vehicle and in the area that you are going to occupy in the next 10-20 seconds. This is a good minimum distance to be visually searching ahead of your vehicle for hazardous situations.

2. Search for:

- **Pedestrians**
- **Animals**
- **Children**
- **Blind spots** (parked vehicles or obstacles that you cannot see around)
- **Cyclists**
- **Any other hazards that could cause a collision or an emergency response if it's not identified early.**

3. When traveling in urban areas, the width of the area you should be studying is from the building on your left to the building on your right. This allows you to study the sidewalks (with the pedestrians), any vehicles or cyclists on the roadway and any vehicles parked on the sides of the road.

Visual Search: City

Proper visual searching in cities can help the defensive driver avoid collisions.

4. When traveling in rural areas, the width of the area you should be studying is from fence to fence or from tree-line to tree-line in areas that are not fenced. This will take into account the shoulders of the road as well as drainage areas and ditches.

Visual Search: Country

Visually searching from fence line to fence line on rural roadways allows the defensive driver to identify and respond to potential hazards before they become emergency situations.

Tip 13
Worst Case Scenario

13. Anticipate the worst-case scenario

"Expect others to do the wrong thing. That way, all of your surprises will be pleasant ones."

When you identify a potential hazard ask yourself, "What is the worst thing that this hazard could do that might involve me in a crash?" Then, take whatever action is necessary to remove that hazardous situation. Time and time again, the most frequent action that you will take is to simply slow down and let the situation unfold ahead of you while leaving yourself plenty of time to respond. You may also need to change lanes to provide yourself with an extra space cushion and additional response time. Chances are, the worst-case scenario will not occur. In those situations, you can be thankful and continue to search for other potential hazards. However, on those occasions when the worst-case action does occur, you have already given yourself more opportunity to avoid a collision and have reduced the amount of stress to yourself because you had already anticipated that situation.

Tip 14

Respond...
Don't React

14. Respond before you have to react

You have probably heard it said that it is better to be proactive than it is to be reactive. This is definitely the case when you are operating a motor vehicle. Being proactive means that you are taking the steps necessary to avoid hazardous situations before they become situations in which you have no choice but to react. On the road, these reactions are often emergency maneuvers like sudden braking or swerving to avoid a collision. Maintaining a safe following distance and developing the habit of searching well down the road for potential hazards are two techniques that enable defensive drivers to avoid react-only situations.

Did you know?

Many crashes occur when drivers get into react-only situations and either choose the wrong action or find that there is not enough reaction time to avoid the collision.

Tip 15
Target Point

15. Keep your vehicle centered in its lane of travel

One of the fundamental concepts in vehicle control is identifying a "Target" or "Target Point" that you can "Aim" at with your vehicle. This concept is really quite basic, but has seldom been explained to drivers. The concept is: your body goes where your eyes are looking. See, I told you it was simple. Think about it, what happens when a driver looks over his left shoulder? Typically, his vehicle starts to drift to the left, where his eyes are looking. The same thing happens when a driver is looking over his right shoulder, talking to the passengers (or yelling at the kids) in the back seat. The vehicle often starts to drift

to the right, again where the driver's eyes are looking. This reaction is simply based upon how the human mind and body work together. The same thing happens even when a person is not driving a vehicle. Think about shooting an arrow at a target. You want to hit the center of the target, so that is where you focus your attention, on the bull's eye. Consider how hard it would be to hit the bull's eye if you were focusing on a point to the right or left of the target. Here's another example: you are at a fair and decide that you want to win a stuffed animal at one of those baseball throwing target booths. For two dollars you get three chances to knock down the milk bottles stacked on top of each other. You pay your money and the person behind the counter hands you your three baseballs. You pick up the first ball, and where do you look? Exactly, you focus your attention on the center of the three milk bottles. That is the "Target Point" you need to hit in order to knock down the bottles and begin your journey toward that giant stuffed puppy dog.

The technique for keeping your vehicle centered while driving works the same way, only instead of a bull's eye or stuffed animal, your reward is decreasing the likelihood of a crash by keeping your vehicle centered in its lane of travel. To do this, you find a Target Point well ahead of your vehicle that is centered in your lane of travel. It could be a tree, the corner of a building or even a light post. The important thing is that it's a stationary object that is directly in the center of your desired lane of travel. Now, you simply aim your vehicle at that Target Point. This will help you center your vehicle in your lane of travel and keep you from drifting from side to side in your lane. You do not stare at this Target Point, but you include it in your visual scan to confirm that you are still on track.

This "Target Point" concept has other benefits as well:

1. It helps keep your eyes up and looking ahead of your vehicle so you can actively search for potential hazards.

2. It helps you see what is happening in and beyond upcoming corners.

3. It helps you stay aware of changing situations ahead of your vehicle since you will be continually changing your Target Point as your path of travel changes (after going around corners, over hills, etc.).

Tip 16
Train

16. Train yourself and others

Most of the learning models in use today tell us that one of the best ways for anyone, especially adults, to learn is to explain a concept to someone else. Driving SMART is no exception, and it has multiple benefits:

1. It gives you a chance to reinforce your own training in the concepts of SMART Driving.

2. It gives you the chance to help someone else become a safer, more informed driver.

3. It gives you a tactful way to work with a driver that you are uncomfortable riding with. Think about it, how do you tell someone that you think he is an unsafe driver? Many times, you wouldn't even mention this to a friend or co-worker because you don't want to embarrass him or make him upset. However, if you say: "Hey, I recently read a book about SMART Driving" or "I recently attended a seminar on SMART Driving and I want to tell you what I learned. It will help me reinforce the new concepts." This approach gives you an opportunity to both reinforce your training and, hopefully, to get the other person thinking more about defensive driving. This works especially well if you can give examples of how applying the concepts you learned helped you avoid a collision or made you more confident or comfortable behind the wheel.

Tip 17

Practice Makes Permanent

17. Practice the skills you want to improve

Everybody has strengths and weaknesses when it comes to their driving ability. Identifying the areas that you feel least comfortable with will give you an opportunity to practice those techniques and increase your confidence whenever you are behind the wheel.

For example: Let's say that you don't feel comfortable parallel parking. Get a couple of cardboard boxes or orange cones and set up a simulated parallel parking situation in an empty parking lot.

1. Stop your vehicle next to the spot where you want to park.

2. Set the boxes or cones to the side of your vehicle and in the front and rear of your vehicle (pretend that they are parked vehicles that you have to parallel park in between).

3. Now practice parking your vehicle between the cones/boxes.

4. You can start with a large space between the boxes/cones (about two car lengths) then, as your confidence increases, you can shorten the distance between the obstacles. It helps if you set this parking simulation up with a line or other boundary (curb, edge of parking lot, etc) to the side of your vehicle so you can use this edge to simulate the curb or sidewalk.

5. Practice parallel parking to both the passenger's and driver's sides of your vehicle until you feel comfortable with both maneuvers.

You can also set up simulations for other driving maneuvers you may want to practice. Remember: "Practice Makes Permanent." Practicing your driving skills will help you develop proper driving habits and allow you to increase your proficiency whenever you are in control of a motor vehicle.

Tip 18

Eliminate Distractions

18. Eliminate in-vehicle distractions

Many of the collisions that occur every day can be traced back to one root cause: The driver of a vehicle was distracted from the task of driving. Distractions can come from many sources and can originate both inside and outside of the vehicle. "In-Vehicle" distractions can include: Phone calls, eating, drinking (any beverage), shaving, applying make-up, conversations with passengers, pets in the car, loud music, text messaging (really, some people actually send

Cell Phone Driver

Thousands of crashes occur every day when drivers make bad choices about distracted driving.

text messages while they are driving), smoking, navigation systems, and reading (maps, books, reports). Loose items can also shift or be blown around by the wind if a window is open. These are just a few of the distractions that can occur inside a vehicle, there are many more. However, if you look at this list, you will notice that without exception the driver can control, or eliminate, every one of these potential distractions when he is driving. Safe driving is all about choice. A safe driver chooses to eliminate as many distractions as possible from his driving environment. Unsafe drivers choose to allow distractions to prevent them from applying SMART Driving concepts. Eliminating distractions allows the driver to focus his attention where it needs to be focused, on the task of driving. This focus greatly increases the driver's chances of collision-free driving.

Did you know?

Drivers distracted by cell phones have contributed to so many collisions that many states are considering, or have already enacted, laws prohibiting the use of hand-held cell phones while driving.

Tip 19

Toss The Dice!

19. Nothing hanging from the mirror

This is an in-vehicle distraction that is so common I felt it needed its own section. Probably since the first inside, rear view mirror was stuck to the front windshield, drivers have felt the need to hang something from the mirror mount. The next time you are walking through a parking lot, take a look at the rear view mirrors of the vehicles you are passing. You will probably see everything from fuzzy dice and dream catchers to parking permits and air fresheners. Who knows, you may even have one of these items hanging from your own mirror. There are two main reasons why drivers should not have anything hanging from the inside rear view mirror bracket:

1. Anything hanging from the mirror bracket can swing around and distract the driver, causing him to take his eyes off the road.

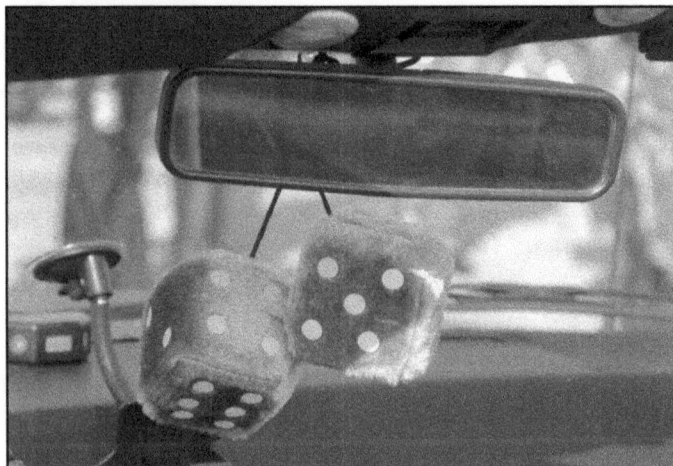

Items hanging from the mirror are not only a visual distraction, they also create an additional blind spot for the driver.

2. Anything hanging down from the mirror bracket will contribute to the natural blind spot that is created by the mirror itself. The next time you are stopped at an intersection waiting for the light to change, take a look and see how much of a blind spot is created by your inside rear view mirror. Most likely, you will notice that pedestrians, cyclists and even vehicles can be hidden in this blind spot. This is especially true for taller drivers or for drivers who have adjusted their seat to a higher position to increase their visibility out of the vehicle. Making sure that there is nothing hanging from the rear view mirror is another one of those choices that is 100% under the control of the driver. Making the choice to remove hanging items is making a choice to drive safer.

Did you know?

There is nothing that a driver can hang from his mirror that is more important than his safety or the safety of other road users.

Tip 20

In The Driver's Seat

20. Be sure to have your driver's seat adjusted properly

Having the seat properly adjusted helps the driver reduce fatigue and increases visibility out of the vehicle. A driver should have his seat adjusted so he can easily reach all of the vehicle's controls and can comfortably drive with both hands on the steering wheel. While on the road, you have probably noticed many motorists who drive with their seats in a semi-reclined position. While some drivers might think this looks "cool," it significantly reduces their ability to visually scan ahead of and around their vehicles. Additionally, it reduces the driver's ability to have both hands on the wheel, thereby reducing his ability to quickly respond to emergency situations.

Tip 21
What's On Your Mind?

21. Communication

As drivers, it is important for us to communicate our intentions to other road users so they can better anticipate our actions. Obviously, the most common forms of communication between road users are a vehicle's turn signals and brake lights. The sole purpose of these devices is to allow the vehicle operator to communicate his intentions to other road users. A vehicle's headlights and horn are also used to communicate with other road users (with varying degrees of tactfulness). There are, however, some other forms of communication that are more subtle. One is the lane position of the vehicle. If a person is approaching an intersection where he has the option of making a right turn and his vehicle is starting to move over toward the right part of his lane of travel, the driver is sending a signal to other road users that he may be getting ready to execute a right turn. Other forms of communication come directly from the driver and include: posture of the driver, eye contact and verbal communication.

Did you know?

If a driver is sending conflicting signals, or no signals at all about his intentions, he is gambling on the ability of other road users to predict his actions.

Tip 22
Keep Your Gestures to Yourself

22. Do not gesture to other drivers at intersections

How many times have you been stopped at a four-way intersection with other vehicles present and gestured to let one of the other motorists know that they could proceed? Many drivers feel that this is

Gestures

Here is a four-way intersection controlled by stop signs. Note how a driver could contribute to a collision by gesturing to another road user.

a courtesy they are showing to other motorists. However, there have been instances where this type of "kindness" has led to litigation. During my research for a training program I was developing, I read about some circumstances where gesturing motorists were actually named as defendants in court cases. According to the documentation, "The Defendant" had gestured to another motorist or pedestrian while stopped in traffic only to have that person be struck by another road user as he entered the roadway. In these cases, the driver who gestured was named in a lawsuit claiming he had contributed to the crash. While the two cases I studied both found that the gesturing driver was not liable (since the driver in both cases was only indicating that <u>he</u> would yield the right-of-way) these drivers still had to go to court and defend their decision to gesture to another road user. The whole situation could have been avoided if the driver had simply continued to yield the right-of-way until the other person proceeded.

Did you know?

A driver is not obligated to gesture to other road users concerning right-of-way.

Tip 23
Active Searching

23. Actively search for hazards

One of the main causes of motor vehicle collisions is inattention by the driver. Many of the collisions that occur every day could be avoided if drivers would simply develop the skill of "active searching." Active searching means just that: active. Rather than simply driving down the road staring straight ahead, a driver is specifically looking for any situation or activity ahead of or around his vehicle that could lead to an emergency situation. Again, this is a relatively simple concept, but it takes practice to develop the habit. The key is to take in as much relevant driving information as possible and ask yourself, "What's wrong with this picture?" and, "What can I see that could potentially contribute to me being involved in a collision if I do not respond beforehand?" Many of the concepts taught in the SMART Driving System™ go hand-in-hand to help increase all around driver safety. For instance, looking well ahead of the vehicle and identifying a target point helps the driver keep his eyes ahead of his vehicle so he can recognize potential hazards. This skill helps with active searching because it requires the driver to look up the road rather than just focusing on the vehicle directly ahead.

Tip 24
Give Yourself Time

24. Give yourself extra time to arrive at your destination

Part of planning ahead involves giving yourself plenty of time to reach your destination. Checking traffic updates can help you plan your route to avoid congested areas. However, traffic reports are not foolproof since changes in traffic conditions can occur at any time. Therefore, it's a good idea to give yourself some extra time to reach your intended destination whenever possible. Simply leaving 10 minutes earlier can help you avoid feeling rushed and will allow you to make adjustments to changing traffic conditions without being tempted to exceed the speed limit or drive in an unsafe manner in order to reach your destination on time. This extra time will also help you reduce or eliminate the stress caused by being late for an appointment.

Tip 25

You Don't Care About My Honor Student?

---

25. Remove bumper/window stickers

Have you ever been behind a vehicle and found yourself squinting to read a bumper sticker? I have. In fact, I have even caught myself edging closer to the vehicle stopped in front of me in traffic in order to read the clever, not so clever, or just plain confusing joke or comment displayed on a bumper sticker. However, as I began to think about factors that could contribute to rear end collisions, I found myself rethinking this activity. One of the bumper stickers that I have often seen reads, "If you can read this bumper sticker, you're too close!" While this is amusing, it is also quite true. The writing on many bumper stickers is so small (to accommodate the limited surface

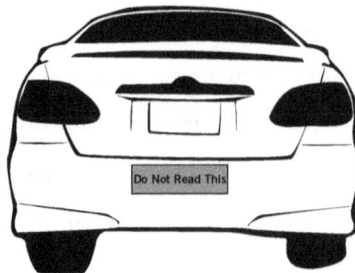

area) that the person behind the vehicle sporting the sticker would have to get much closer than the safe following distance in order to make out the words. Sure, you might think that it only takes a few seconds to read a bumper sticker, but think about it; if you are focusing on reading a bumper sticker, you are not focusing on potential hazards ahead of and around your vehicle.

The same can be said for the person behind you if you are driving a vehicle with a bumper sticker. The person driving the vehicle behind you might be distracted or focusing on your bumper when he should be maintaining a safe following distance and paying attention to what is going on around his vehicle. Window stickers can cause a similar distraction, but they pose an additional hazard as well: obstructing visibility from the vehicle. Many drivers will place a window sticker in the center of their rear window so that it can be easily seen. However, this often places the sticker directly in the line of sight for the rear view mirror and creates additional blind spots.

Tip 26
Relax

26. Reduce stress

This sounds like one of those statements that is easier said than done, but taking steps to reduce your stress level when you are operating a motor vehicle can make you a safer driver. A driver who is stressed out, angry, or driving aggressively is far more likely to be involved in a collision than a driver who is relaxed and focused on driving defensively. Furthermore, a relaxed driver who is not stressed out arrives at his destination in a better frame of mind. The relaxed driver does not have to take extra time to unwind from the rigors of driving once he reaches his destination.

Did you know?

One of the best ways to reduce stress while driving is to make a conscious effort to identify and remove the factor(s) that cause you to be anxious when behind the wheel. Common factors are running late, being unfamiliar with the area, or driving while preoccupied with something else that's going on in your busy day.

Tip 27
Pick The Right Vehicle

27. Compare visibility when selecting a vehicle

People select a vehicle for purchase based on many different criteria including: cost, fuel economy, color, mileage (used vehicle), vehicle condition, maintenance records, style, popularity, and size to name but a few. However, many prospective car buyers do not take the time to critically compare the visibility from the driver's seat. If you are considering the purchase of a vehicle for yourself or for someone else, one of your decision criteria should be visibility. The way to check visibility is to get behind the wheel, adjust the driver's seat and identify the location and size of a vehicle's blind spots. This check should be performed by whoever is going to be operating the vehicle. A visibility check should be an important factor that you consider when purchasing a vehicle.

Tip 28
Ongoing Pre-Trip

28. Preform an ongoing Pre-Trip

One of the other tips in this book is to perform a "Pre-Trip" on a regular basis. The Pre-Trip identifies any maintenance or safety issues that need to be resolved in order to ensure that your vehicle is safe to operate. This vehicle inspection should be scheduled and be performed in a consistent manner every time.

Reflection Check

Any reflective surface can be used to verify that your headlights are working. Many times you can view your vehicle's reflection from a parking space.

Another way to monitor your vehicle in the time between scheduled inspections is to perform what I like to call an ongoing Pre-Trip. Some of this inspection can even be performed from the driver's seat without having to leave the vehicle. While parked in your garage with the door closed, you turn on your headlights and verify that both are working (high and low beam) by looking at their reflection on the garage door. You can then turn off your headlights and check your turn signals in the same way. You can also verify that your vehicle's brake lights and back-up lights are working using this technique.

Headlight Check

This photo, taken inside a garage, shows how easy it is to make sure your vehicles headlights are working. Note how the passenger's side headlight is out.

To check your vehicle's back-up lights, set the vehicle's parking brake, turn the ignition key to the "On" position (do not start the vehicle), place the vehicle's gear selector in "Reverse" and take your foot off the brake slowly (to make sure that your parking brake is holding the vehicle securely). You should then be able to see your vehicle's back-up lights reflected on the surface behind your vehicle. You may wish to place a small mirror behind and/or in front of your vehicle to make this process even easier. A driver can also perform this check while stopped at a light in traffic by looking for his vehicle's reflection in the bumper of the vehicle stopped in front of him or by checking his vehicle's reflection in any other reflective surface (like the windows of a building across the intersection).

Tip 29
What Are You Looking At?

29. Move your point of concentration every two to three seconds

Have you ever arrived at a destination and not remembered the drive that brought you there? Called "Automatic Driving" by some, this phenomenon can occur when the driver is just going through the motions of driving and is distracted, fatigued, or just "driving on autopilot" rather than actively searching ahead of and around his vehicle. An excellent way to eliminate automatic driving, and to help keep yourself alert, is to move your point of concentration every two to three seconds while driving. Moving your point of concentration is different than simply moving your eyes. It is the key component of active searching. Using this principle, you move your point of concentration by focusing on what you are seeing when you move your eyes every two to three seconds. The technique is designed to increase the driver's risk perception while he is driving. To help understand this concept, it is important to explain the difference between sight and perception. For the purpose of defensive driving, I define sight as the information that is transmitted to a person's brain by his eyes.

Perception occurs when a person actually registers what his eyes are showing him and makes driving decisions based upon the relevant information he perceives.

For example: A driver may *see* a group of pedestrians standing at an upcoming intersection, but *perception* doesn't occur until the driver moves his point of concentration to the pedestrians to verify that they are staying put and that no one is entering the roadway. This perception allows the driver to determine to what extent an emergency situation could develop based upon his perception of the risk presented by the pedestrians.

Moving your point of concentration every two to three seconds allows you to gather as much relevant information as possible about what is going on ahead of and around your vehicle. It also helps keep you alert and can help you avoid the trap of automatic driving.

Tip 30

Closer Than They Appear

30. Check your mirrors every five to eight seconds

In order to know what is going on beside and behind your vehicle, you need to develop the habit of checking your mirrors frequently. Checking your mirrors every five to eight seconds will allow you to gather much needed information about what is happening, and what is going to happen, in the space around your vehicle. Developing the habit of frequently checking your mirrors allows you to anticipate and respond to the changes that are occurring beside and behind your vehicle before they become emergency situations. This habit is one of the most difficult to develop. Even when I work with professional drivers, I find that many have not developed the habit of checking their mirrors every five to eight seconds. They understand and admit the importance of this technique, but it takes a conscious effort to actually develop the habit. If a driver is actively searching for potential hazards and is moving his point of concentration every two to three seconds, he needs to make sure that he is including his mirrors in his visual search pattern.

Did you know?

If a driver is not actively checking his mirrors on a regular basis, he has no idea of what's happening beside and behind his vehicle.

Tip 31
Foot on Brake = Eyes on Mirror

31. Check your rear view mirrors every time you apply the brake

Another good habit to develop is checking your rear view mirrors every time you put your foot on the brake. This will allow you to see what is happening directly behind your vehicle. It will help you determine if the vehicle behind you is slowing down or if you need to change lanes to avoid being struck from behind. Even once you come to a stop, it's a good idea to continue checking what's happening behind your vehicle. You should also try to see behind the vehicle stopped directly behind you. This may give you a chance to move and avoid being struck from behind if the vehicle behind you is rear-ended. I watched the interview of a man who was stopped behind a big truck on the highway when his vehicle was struck from behind by another large truck. The video showed the aftermath of the collision and the vehicle the man was driving. The vehicle had been struck so hard from behind that you could not even see it between the two trucks. The two trucks were actually touching each other and had to be pulled apart by a tow truck. Amazingly, the man in the vehicle that was crushed lived and escaped with relatively minor injuries. During the interview, the man said that he saw the truck coming up behind him and knew that he was going to be involved in a crash. I often wonder if the man had not given himself enough space between his vehicle and the truck ahead of him to provide an escape path that would have allowed him to pull away and avoid the crash altogether.

Eyes on Mirror

Checking the rear view mirrors allows the defensive driver to verify that the vehicles to the rear are stopping.

Tip 32

Whose Turn Is It Anyway?

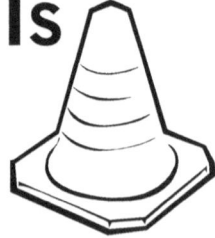

32. When in doubt, yield the right of way

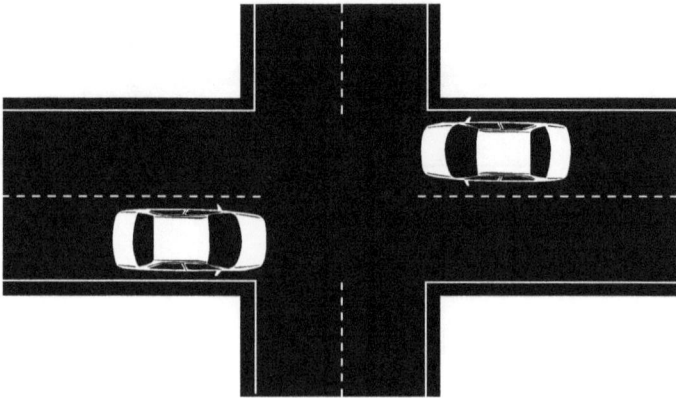

Knowing the rules of the road is a good idea for any motorist. It will make you a more knowledgeable and, presumably, safer driver. It can also help you avoid getting traffic citations for failing to obey a law that you were unsure of. One area of the law that every motorist should understand is the section that addresses yielding the right-of-way at intersections.

Typically, if you find yourself at a four-way intersection with other vehicles, the first vehicle to arrive at the intersection and come to a complete stop has the right-of-way. If two vehicles stop at the same time, typically the vehicle to the right has the right-of-way. If the vehicles stop at the same time and are directly across from each other at the intersection, both can proceed at the same time, unless one of the vehicles is turning across the path of the other vehicle (which is going straight). In that situation, the vehicle going straight has the right-of-way and the turning vehicle is required to yield.

However, I would suggest that you check the regulations for your own state to verify that these are the laws for your area. If you find yourself at an intersection and you are unsure about who has the right-of-way, you should yield on the side of safety and allow the other vehicle to proceed. You will lose far less time than you would if you were involved in an intersection collision because you thought the other motorist was going to yield.

Tip 33
The Setup

33. Make any necessary adjustments before you start driving

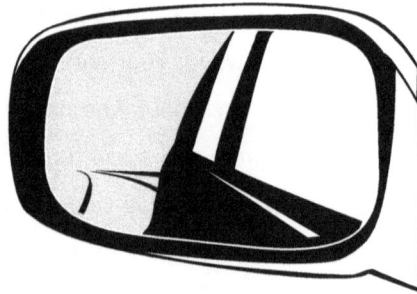

Before you start the vehicle and begin driving, make sure that you have made any necessary adjustments to your vehicle. It is always safer to make these adjustments while you are stopped, before your tires start to roll. These changes can include adjustments to the seat, mirrors, tilt steering wheel, head rest, seat belt height, volume of stereo, arm rests, and climate control.

If a driver does not make these adjustments while the vehicle is stopped, he may choose to do so while he is driving and this activity can be a major distraction.

Tip 34
The New Ride

34. Familiarize yourself with any new vehicle

Anytime you drive an unfamiliar vehicle (new, mom's, friend's, company's, rental car, etc.) it's a good idea to take a few minutes to familiarize yourself with that vehicle. Located the controls for the headlights, windshield wipers, climate control and cruise control as well as any other controls that you may need to use while you are operating that vehicle. You should also familiarize yourself with that vehicle's blind spots and visibility characteristics before you get out on the road. Make sure that you have the mirrors and seat adjusted properly and that there are no warning lights still illuminated after the engine is running. These lights may indicate that the vehicle needs service.

Getting to know the vehicle becomes even more important if you are going to be driving that vehicle in an unfamiliar area. This can increase the chances that you may be distracted and lead to an increased stress level, both of which could contribute to you being involved in a collision.

Tip 35
Leave The T-Bones For The Barbecue

35. Clear intersections before entering

Intersection collisions are often the most severe and costly because of the forces involved when two vehicles traveling in different directions collide. Anytime you are approaching an intersection, you should "clear" that intersection by looking to the left, front, right, front and then back to the left. This five-point check is used to verify that traffic that is supposed to stop has stopped. You want to check to the left first as you approach because that is the direction of the most immediate danger. You want to check to the left last to be sure that nothing has

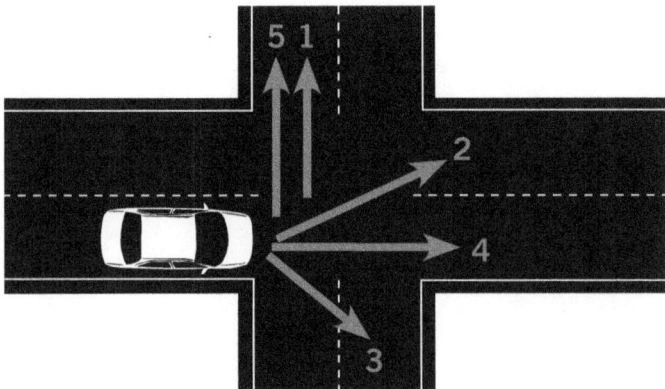

changed since you first cleared that side. The key is to focus your point of concentration and actively search for hazards, not just go through the motions of clearing the intersection. You want to clear the intersection before you enter. If you wait too long, and another motorist fails to obey his traffic signal, all you will see is the vehicle that is about to collide with your vehicle and you will not have time to avoid the crash.

Did you know?

In 2006, over 2.4 million crashes occurred in or near intersections in the United States.

NHTSA : Traffic Safety Facts 2006

Tip 36
The Inevitability of Change

36. Anticipate changes at intersections

Anytime you approach an intersection, you should be expecting the conditions to change. Intersections are, by design, locations where changes occur. Vehicles slow, stop, turn, accelerate and cross travel paths. It is also the area where pedestrians are most likely to be crossing the roadway. By planning ahead and studying the area you are going to occupy in the next 10 to 20 seconds, you can better anticipate what changes are likely to occur in the intersection before you arrive.

Intersections

As you approach any intersection, study the situation and anticipate changing conditions.

Tip 37
Play By The Rules

37. Study the rules of the road – don't gamble with your driving record

A big part of avoiding traffic tickets is understanding the regulations for your area. Obviously, speed zones and traffic lights send the same message no matter where you are, but there are other regulations that vary from state to state and even city to city. If you find yourself in a situation where you do not know what is legally allowed, look up the regulation in your state's traffic codebook. This book is available from the Department of Motor Vehicles (DMV) and may be available to view or download at the DMV Website. The online PDF version is nice because it allows the user to perform a keyword search for specific regulations. It's a good idea to check these regulations, because this is the same information used by law enforcement to regulate traffic offenses. Knowing and following the regulations will greatly reduce the chances that you will find yourself in a situation where you are telling a police officer, "I didn't know I couldn't do that."

Tip 38
Goodbye Hazards

38. Remove hazards whenever possible

Hazards can occur both inside and outside the vehicle. In-vehicle distractions can be managed or eliminated by the driver to help reduce the hazards they pose. However, there are many hazards that occur outside the vehicle that a driver may also be able to remove. Some may be found on a driver's own property. Tall plants can obstruct a driver's vision or prevent other drivers from seeing him exiting his driveway. These plants and shrubs can be trimmed back or removed. Additionally, any other type of visual obstruction (fencing, retaining walls, parked vehicles) should be removed or relocated to help provide drivers with clear lines of sight.

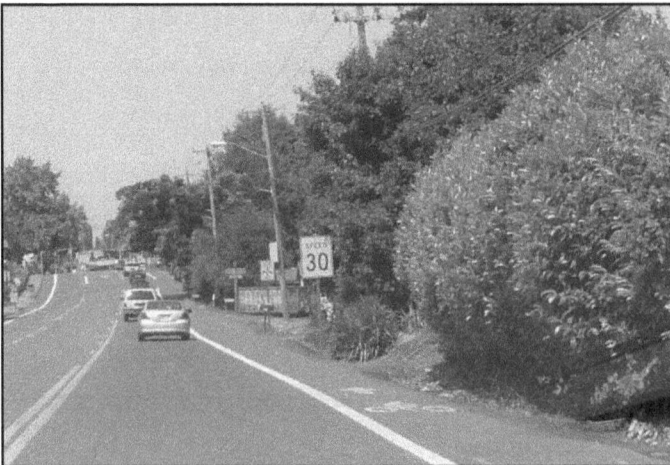

Driveway Hazard

Note how the trees and bushes along the right side of this road obstruct the view into and out of the driveways.

Tip 39
Tell Somebody

39. Communicate hazards to others

Letting other people know about the hazards that you have identified can also help reduce crashes. Telling your family and friends about hazards that you have identified can reduce the chance that they will be affected by those hazards when they are driving. If you identify a hazard that obstructs your vision or causes a distraction, you may want to report that hazard to the property owner and see if he will remove it. There may be a reason that the hazard cannot be removed, or the property owner may say "no," but you never know until you ask. If you do not wish to speak with the property owner, you can notify the city of the potential hazard. The city can then investigate the issue and may ask or instruct the home owner to remove the hazard.

Tip 40
Not So Close

40. Maintain a safe following distance

Following Distance

Maintaining proper following distance (in this case six seconds from the vehicle ahead) allows the driver to perform a better visual search and gives him enough time to respond to any action the vehicle ahead may take.

A person operating a vehicle has the most control over the space directly in front of his vehicle. With that in mind, a driver should always try to maintain a safe following distance between his vehicle and the vehicle directly ahead. Ideally, a driver should try to maintain at least four seconds of following distance when he is traveling at speeds below 30 MPH. At speeds above 30 MPH, a driver should try to maintain at least six seconds of following distance. This distance allows the driver to respond to changing situations ahead of his vehicle without having to make the sudden, emergency maneuvers often made by drivers who are following too closely. In addition, this following distance allows the driver to see what is happening further up the road. A driver who is following too closely has to focus more of his attention on the vehicle directly ahead. This prevents the tailgating driver from identifying potentially hazardous situations ahead of his vehicle.

How does a driver calculate his following distance in seconds?

The technique is really quite simple:
When the vehicle ahead of you passes a stationary object or point on the road, you begin to count. However many seconds it takes you to reach that same point equals your following distance. Remember this fact: A vehicle traveling at 60 MPH travels the length of a football field every 3.4 seconds.

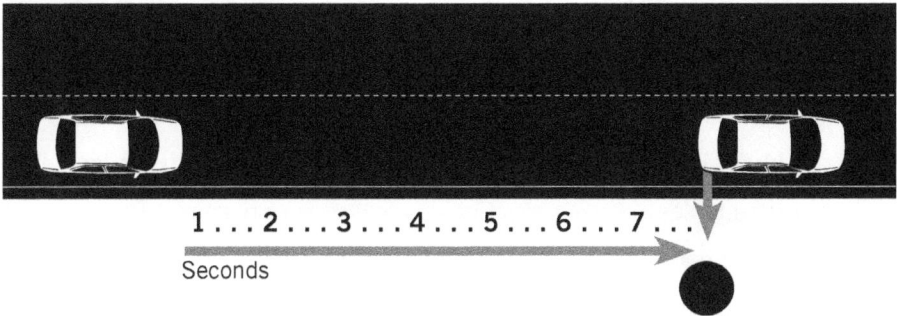

1 . . . 2 . . . 3 . . . 4 . . . 5 . . . 6 . . . 7 . . .

Seconds

Tip 41
All Clear?

41. Check around your vehicle before you enter

While you are walking up to your vehicle, you have an excellent opportunity to perform a visual check to make sure that there are no issues of concern. Many self-defense classes suggest that people use this technique to check for potential threats from criminals, but it works equally well to spot fluid leaks, toys, pets or kids that may have crawled underneath your vehicle while it was parked.

Obviously the higher your vehicle sits off the ground, the easier it will be for you to see underneath. This is also a good time to look at the tires to see if they are noticeably low on air pressure. This is one of those habits that doesn't take any extra time to perform, but can save time, money, and possibly lives, in the long-run.

I remember a story I heard on a voice mail when I worked for UPS about a child that got stuck underneath a vehicle while the driver was away making a delivery. The little boy had crawled underneath the UPS truck to retrieve a toy. While trying to extract his toy, his shirt became caught on a part of the vehicle's undercarriage and he could not get out. Meanwhile, the driver had completed his delivery and was heading back to continue his delivery route. He climbed into his truck and was about to start the engine when he heard a voice yelling out, "Time-out mister!! Time-out mister!!" The driver got out and discovered the child trapped underneath his vehicle. This story had a happy ending, but it could have ended tragically had the child not called out before the engine started. Checking underneath and around your vehicle as you approach can help a you avoid similar situations.

Check Behind Vehicle

This is another example of why it is a good idea to back into parking spaces. Simply making sure that there is nothing or no one behind your vehicle before backing up can save a life.

Tip 42
Be Ready To Go

42. Have your key ready when you get to your vehicle

This is a safety tip used by personal safety consultants, but it's also a good driving safety tip. As you are approaching your vehicle, you should already have your key in hand. This will allow you to use the time it takes you to reach your vehicle to check around it for potential hazards and oncoming traffic. A driver who is distracted by digging in his/her pocket or purse trying to locate keys may not notice a potential hazard (like an approaching vehicle or cyclist).

Additionally, once you get into your vehicle, you should minimize the time spent before you drive away. The longer you wait inside your vehicle before driving away, the more likely it is that the situation around your vehicle will have changed from when you last checked. If you have your key ready when you get to your vehicle, you can get in and drive away sooner, and more safely, than a driver who is taking extra time searching for his keys.

Tip 43
Do The Windows

43. Keep your windows clean both inside and out

This is another one of those safety tips that sounds very basic, but there are a lot of people driving around with dirty windows. Quite simply, dirty windows limit visibility into and out of the vehicle. Having the inside of your windows clean helps reduce glare and improves your visibility out of the vehicle. The safety benefits here are obvious: the better you can see out of your vehicle, the more information you can gather about what is going on around your vehicle.

Visibility into your vehicle is important because other road users will often be looking into your vehicle to try to determine your intentions as a motorist. If these other road users are unable to make eye contact with you or to see what you are doing or where you are looking, they will have to try to predict what you are going to do. In essence, they will be guessing at your intentions. The danger is that they may guess wrong and the result could lead to a collision.

Tip 44
Sleep It Off

44. Get plenty of rest -
DO NOT drive when drowsy

Fatigue is one of the major causes of motor vehicle crashes. It is difficult to get an accurate account of the total number of crashes that occur each year as a result of fatigue. This is mainly due to the fact that many drivers will not admit that they were fatigued prior to their crash. Adding to the difficulty of obtaining an accurate number is the multitude of crashes that occur when fatigue is an unrecognized factor.

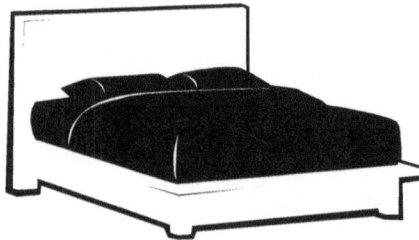

For example: Someone pulls out into the flow of traffic without noticing an oncoming vehicle and is struck by that vehicle. Obviously, the person who pulled his vehicle out into oncoming traffic failed to notice the other vehicle or misjudged the speed of that other vehicle. However, further investigation of the collision may reveal that the person who pulled out was fatigued and was not alert enough to make an accurate determination of what was happening around his vehicle.

The good news is that fatigue is something that can be controlled by the driver. Getting plenty of rest and taking steps to make sure that you remain alert when you are behind the wheel will greatly reduce the likelihood that fatigue will contribute to you being involved in a crash.

Did you know?

According to estimates from the National Highway Traffic Safety Administration, drowsy driving contributes to at least 100,000 police-reported crashes and 1,550 deaths every year in the US.

Tip 45
Out With The Old
In With The New

45. New vs. Old traffic signals

When you are approaching an intersection that is controlled by a traffic light, you need to determine if the traffic light is "New" or if it is an "Old" signal. A "New" signal is one that you observed changing from red to green. Having observed this change, you should be able to better anticipate when the green signal will change to yellow. A traffic signal is considered "Old" if it is already green when it enters your field of view. Since this signal has already changed from red to green, you may not be sure about when it will change to yellow. Obviously, a new signal is better; however, there are some other indicators that can help you determine when an "Old" green light will change to yellow.

One of these indicators is the crosswalk signal for the pedestrian traffic that is traveling in the same direction as your vehicle. If the pedestrian signal is still indicating that it is safe for pedestrians to cross (a walk signal) then it is most likely that the traffic signal you are approaching has been green for only a short time. If the pedestrian signal is flashing the "Do Not Cross" signal or is a flashing red hand, then it's likely that your green light is about to change to yellow. Some of the newer pedestrian crossing signals are equipped with a visual countdown to let the pedestrian traffic know how long they have to cross the intersection. These types of count down signals can be used by a driver to help determine when his green light will likely be changing to yellow. Even pedestrian crosswalk signals without countdown timers can be useful if you pay attention to how many times the red hand or "Do Not Cross" indicator flashes before it becomes solid. In many cities, crosswalk signal indicators are set to flash the same number of times (for a certain length of time) before the lights go solid. If you see the crosswalk indicator change from

"Walk" to a flashing hand or "Do Not Cross" indicator, you can count the number of flashes before the indicator goes solid and determine if there is a set pattern for the crosswalk signals in your area. While this is not guaranteed to work in every city or in every area of the same city, it can provide the driver with additional information about when his green light might be changing to yellow.

Another indicator a driver can use to help determine how long the light ahead has been green is checking the number of vehicles stopped by red lights at the intersection he is approaching. The more vehicles that are stopped and waiting for your green light to turn red, the longer your light has been green, therefore, the sooner it should be changing to yellow.

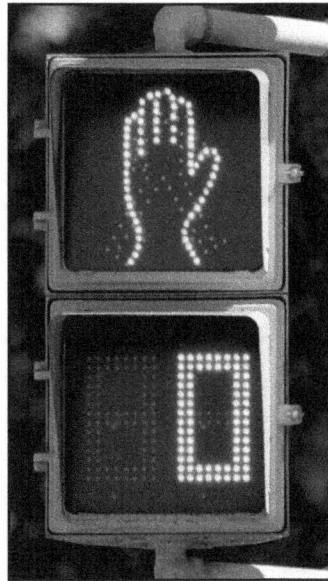

Crossing Signal

A SMART driver can use pedestrian crossing signals to help anticipate when upcoming traffic signals will change.

Tip 46
Point of Commitment

---

46. Visualize your Point of Commitment before entering intersections

The "Point of Commitment" is just what it sounds like. It is the point on the road where your vehicle is committed to proceed through the intersection regardless of what color is displayed on the traffic signal. It's that point where, if the light changes from green to yellow before you reach it, you will still be able to safely stop before you enter the intersection. If the light changes to yellow after you reach your point of commitment, you will have to proceed through the intersection because you would not be able to safely stop your vehicle without entering the intersection.

The important thing to remember is that you are responsible for determining your point of commitment. If you select the wrong point, you will find yourself entering the intersection as the light turns red, which could result in a collision and/or a traffic citation. You will know that you have chosen the right point of commitment if you are able to continue through the intersection at your same, legal speed without passing under a red light.

Tip 47
It's All About The Routine

47. Have a set routine and follow that routine to develop safe driving habits

One of the best ways to develop good driving habits is to establish a good routine and follow that routine whenever possible.

For example:

1. Keep the keys for your vehicle in the same place in your house (that way you will not get frustrated and run late trying to find them).

2. When you park your vehicle, put your key(s) in the same pocket in your clothes or purse (you will not have to check multiple pockets upon your return).

3. Have your vehicle's key in hand before you get to the vehicle.

4. When you are approaching your vehicle, check to be sure that there are no obstructions to the front, rear or underneath.

5. Always put your seat belt on before you start your vehicle.

6. Anytime you find yourself driving a vehicle that someone else has recently driven, check your adjustments (seat, mirrors, headrest, stereo, climate control, etc.) before you start the engine.

Tip 48

Do As I Say...
And As I Do

48. Set a good example

This is a good concept to apply at all times, but especially if you have passengers who are just learning to drive or who are soon-to-be drivers. One of the primary ways they will learn is by watching the way you operate a vehicle. This can be beneficial to their driving skills, or it can cause problems for them depending upon the example you are setting. Some drivers habitually follow too closely to the vehicle ahead or stop too closely to the vehicle ahead of them in traffic. Others do not come to a complete stop at a stop sign or are constantly exceeding the speed limit. Passengers pick up on these habits and make them their own when they are behind the wheel.

Did you know?

Many high schools no longer have the funding to provide driver education classes for new drivers. As a result, many new drivers are relying solely on the training and examples they observe when they are passengers.

Tip 49
Escape Path

49. Leave yourself a way out of an emergency situation

So what should a driver do when the emergency situation occurs? One thing he can do to help reduce the likelihood of a crash is use an escape path. An escape path is simply a path of open space where he can maneuver his vehicle to avoid the collision. The escape path may be the shoulder of the road, the open median or an open lane of travel next to the lane his vehicle currently occupies. Developing the habit of identifying and maintaining an escape path whenever possible gives the driver a safe place to go to avoid crashes caused by the unsafe actions of other road users.

Escape Path

The vehicle on the left of this photo has an open lane (escape path) to the right. There is also an open median to the left that could be used in an emergency situation.

Tip 50
The Old Standby

50. Drive at a legal safe speed

Surprise, surprise! What type of driving safety book would this be if one of the techniques was not the old standby of "Don't speed?" Here we are again talking about personal choice. The driver of a vehicle has to choose if he is going to travel at a safe speed or not. If he chooses, he can exceed the speed limit, or the safe speed for the given roadway conditions, at any time. Unfortunately, many drivers habitually choose to exceed the posted speed limits. Some drivers are so accustomed to exceeding the speed limit that they actually become angry when they are "forced to drive slow" because they get "stuck" behind someone who is not speeding.

Most speeding drivers only worry about the speeding ticket they are likely to receive, not the increased potential for a crash. Data from recent studies, however, suggest that speeders have much more to worry about than a mere fine. According to a report published in January 2008 by the Insurance Institute for Highway Safety (IIHS), police reports listed speed as a contributing factor in about 32% of the fatal traffic crashes that occurred in the United States in 2006. According to that report, 13,500 fatalities were attributed to these crashes. It begs the question how many lives could be saved every year if drivers would simply slow down and drive at a safe speed.

THAT'S A WRAP!

So there you have it. 50 tips that can help keep you, your employees and your loved-ones safer behind the wheel. Every driver has the ability to apply any or all of these tips whenever he is driving. As with anything new, it may take some concentration and diligence at the beginning. But over time these techniques can become habits that a driver will perform without even having to think about it. After all, what is a habit but something a person can do without having to think about it first? Take putting on a seat belt for example: if it's a habit, the seat belt goes on every time. You don't even have to think about it. Before the wheels start to turn, the belt is on. Sometimes, you may not even remember putting on your seat belt, but you feel "weird" if you are driving, or riding as a passenger, and the seat belt is not fastened.

Our driving habits are developed by the choices that we make everyday. Some are good choices and others are not so good. We can choose to identify bad driving habits and try to change them. We can identify a new driving technique and choose to apply it until it becomes a habit. We can choose to eliminate distractions and give ourselves more focus on the road. Or we can choose to tell ourselves that everything is fine and that we don't have any room for improvement when it comes to driving.

It's all a matter of choice ... and the choice is now yours.

www.ingramcontent.com/pod-product-compliance
Lightning Source LLC
Chambersburg PA
CBHW032106080426
42733CB00006B/439